Second Edition

Greenman and the Magic Forest

T0349650

Forest Fun Activity Book B
Susannah Reed

Contents

Welcome to Forest School! ...... page 2

Unit 1  .... page 4

Unit 2 .... page 10

Unit 3 .... page 16

Unit 4 .... page 22

Unit 5 .... page 28

Unit 6 .... page 34

Welcome to Forest School!

Find and colour the animals. Draw you.

Look around you. Find these things and tick (✓).

I am creative.

Now you! Make a collage.

Find and count the objects. Circle the number.

1 / 2

5 / 6

3 / 4

5 / 6

1 / 2

3 / 4

 I am clever.

 Now you! Have a meal outside.

5

Trace and draw the shadows.

I am interested in things.

Now you! Draw your friend's shadow.

Find and circle the day or night animals. Draw another animal.

 I look carefully.

Now YOU! **Find day or night animals.**

Find and colour beautiful things. Draw what they can see.

 I love nature.

 Now you! Look for surprising things in nature.

Look, think and colour.

I care for plants.

NOW YOU!

Plant a sunflower.

Look around you. Find these things and tick (✓).

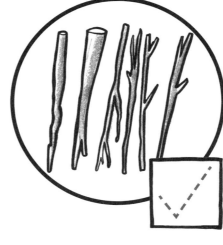

10

 I am creative.

 Now you!

 **Make a tree door.**

Look. Where are these things? Draw.

I can do it.

Now you! Draw a treehouse.

Find six differences. Circle.

 I am clever.

 Now you! Experiment with water.

Find and circle the animals in the forest. Draw the missing animals.

I look carefully.

 Look for animals outside.

Trace and draw you. Find and colour six rabbits.

14

I feel good.

NOW YOU! Do some yoga.

Help the mouse find its home. Colour the animals that make the mouse scared.

 I am kind.

 Now you! Find an animal's home.

Look around you. Find these things and tick (✓).

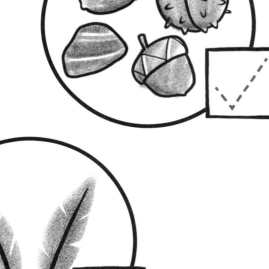

16

I work in a group.

Now you!

Make a forest shop.

Join the numbers to draw mountains. Draw you.

1 2 3 4 5 6

I feel calm.

Now you! 🙂 Do some yoga.

Find and circle the animals. Draw another animal.

 18

 I can do it.

 Make binoculars and watch animals.

Find these things. Draw the patterns.

 I look carefully.

 Now You! Find more patterns in nature.

Follow the road through the town to the fire. Find and circle the animals.

Practise

I am helpful.

NOW YOU!

Play a game of 'Find the toys'.

20

Number the pictures in order. Draw you.

 **I care for my friends.**

Now you! ☺ **Help a friend.**

Unit 4

Think and tick (✓) or cross (✗).

I care for the environment.

Now you! Look after your playground.

Look around you. Find these things and tick (✓).

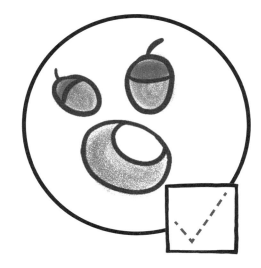

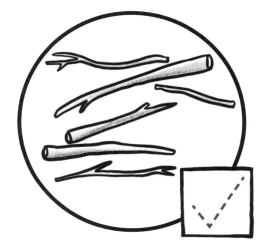

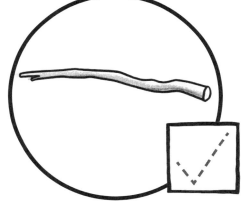

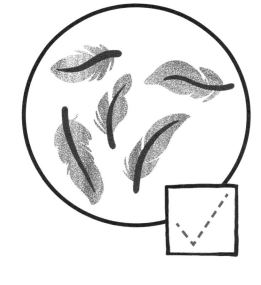

 I can do it.

Now you! Make a wind chime.

Find five differences. Circle. Draw one more.

 24

I am interested in things.

 Now you! Play loud and quiet music.

Match the animals to their homes. Draw the animals.

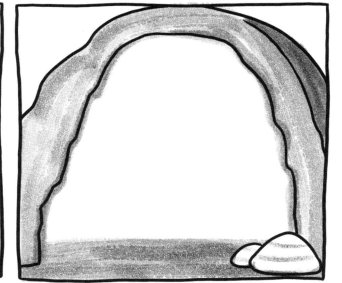

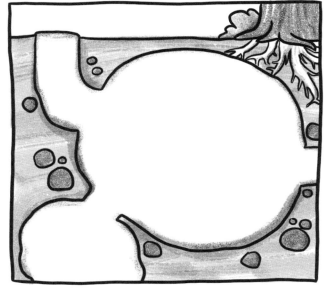

♡ **I care for animals.**

Now you! 😊 **Look for places animals live.**

25

Look and count. Trace and write the numbers.

3 5 6 8

26

☆ I am clever.

Now you! Make dominoes and play a game.

Think and draw the weather.

 I use my senses.

 **Investigate the weather.**

Find and count the animals. Write the numbers.

|  bear | 2 | monkey | | lizard | | bat | |

I look carefully.

 Now you!

Make an animal hiding place.

Look around you. Find these things and tick (✓).

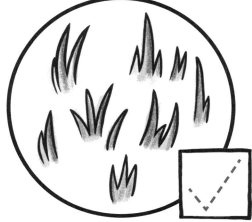

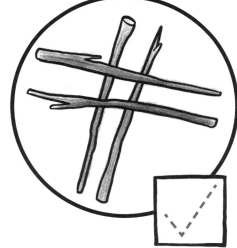

 **I have good ideas.**

 **Make an animal habitat.**

Look and match. Draw one more animal.

30

⭐ **I can do it.**

Now you!  **Make an animal painting.**

Trace the bone. Draw you. Draw what makes you happy.

I feel happy.

Now You! Do some yoga.

31

Think and draw a game.

I have fun with my friends.

Now you!

Play a game with your friends.

Think and match. Draw another animal and its food.

 I am interested in things.

 **Now you!** **Find out more about what animals eat.**

33

Colour the food from plants. Draw the missing food.

34

I look carefully.

Now you!

Find some food from a plant.

Think and draw 😊 or 🙁. Draw food you like.

I like healthy food.

 **Now You!** 😊 **Go shopping for food.**

Look around you. Find these things and tick (✓).

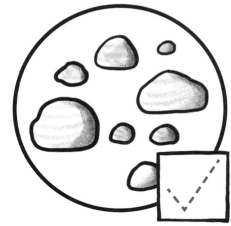

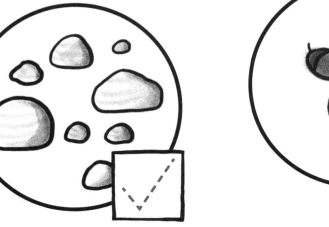

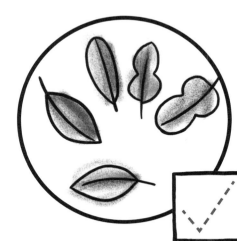

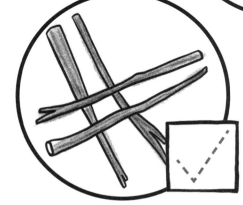

I care for animals.

Now you! Make a bee water station.

36

Look and draw what's missing.

 I care for my friends.

Now you!  Have a picnic with your friends.

Follow, count and colour the corn. Write the number.

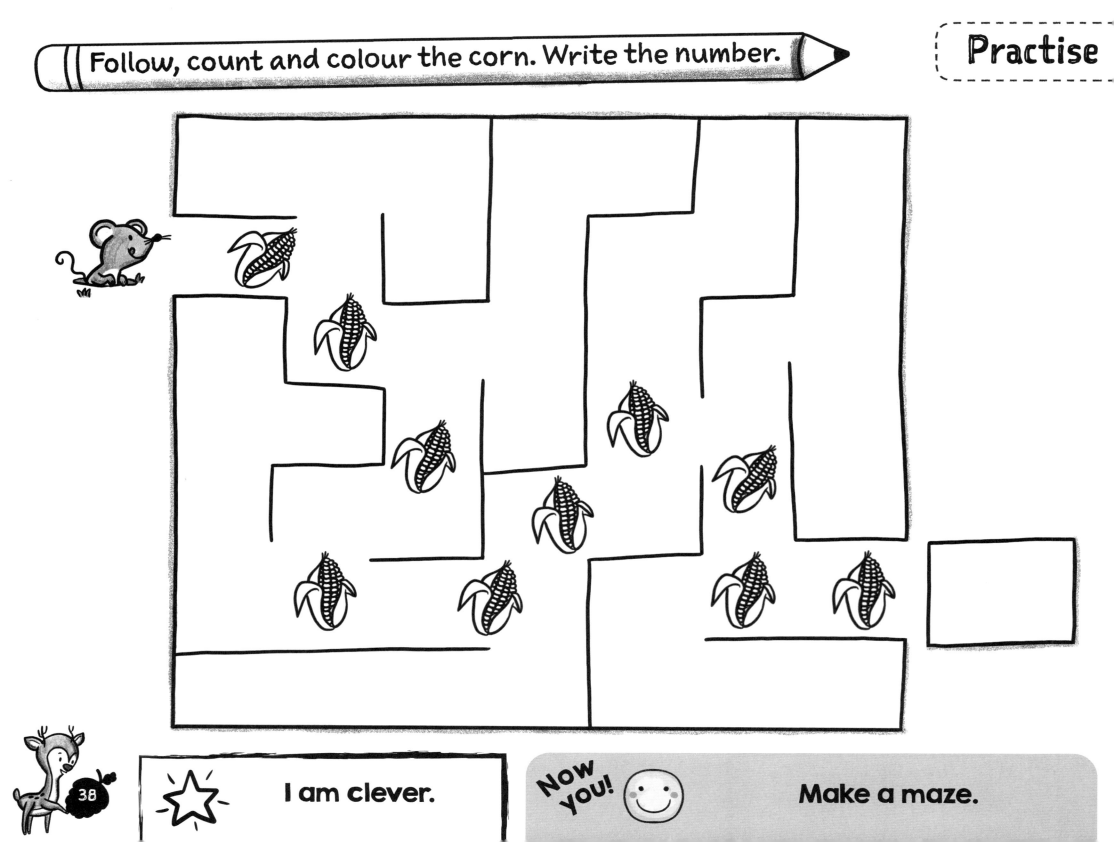

I am clever.

Now you! Make a maze.

Number the pictures in order.

 I am interested in things.

 Now You! **Grow a food plant.**

39

CAMBRIDGE
UNIVERSITY PRESS & ASSESSMENT

Shaftesbury Road, Cambridge CB2 8EA, United Kingdom

One Liberty Plaza, 20th Floor, New York, NY 10006, USA

477 Williamstown Road, Port Melbourne, VIC 3207, Australia

314–321, 3rd Floor, Plot 3, Splendor Forum, Jasola District Centre, New Delhi – 110025, India

103 Penang Road, #05–06/07, Visioncrest Commercial, Singapore 238467

José Abascal, 56–1°, 28003 Madrid, Spain

Cambridge University Press & Assessment is a department of the University of Cambridge.

We share the University's mission to contribute to society through the pursuit of education, learning and research at the highest international levels of excellence.

www.cambridge.org
Information on this title: www.cambridge.org/9781009219259

© Cambridge University Press & Assessment 2023

First published 2015
Second edition 2023

20 19 18 17 16 15 14 13 12 11 10 9 8 7 6 5 4 3

Printed in Poland by Opolgraf

A catalogue record for this publication is available from the British Library

ISBN	978-10-0921-925-9	Activity Book
ISBN	978-10-0921-921-1	Pupil's Book with Pupil's Digital Pack
ISBN	978-10-0921-941-9	Teacher's Book with Teacher's Digital Pack
ISBN	978-10-0921-940-2	Teacher's Book Castellano with Teacher's Digital Pack
ISBN	978-10-0921-946-4	Big Book
ISBN	978-10-0921-943-3	Flashcards
ISBN	978-10-0921-937-2	Classroom Presentation Software
ISBN	978-10-0921-924-2	Pupil's Online Resources
ISBN	978-10-0921-922-8	Home Practice E-book
ISBN	978-10-0921-948-8	Puppet

Acknowledgements

The authors and publishers acknowledge the following sources of copyright material and are grateful for the permissions granted. While every effort has been made, it has not always been possible to identify the sources of all the material used, or to trace all copyright holders. If any omissions are brought to our notice, we will be happy to include the appropriate acknowledgements on reprinting and in the next update to the digital edition, as applicable.

Key: U = Unit.

Cover photography

Vreemous/DigitalVision Vectors

Illustration

Sheila Cabeza de Vaca

Typesetting

Aphik, S.A. de C.V.